SOLVING
CROSS-COUNTRY
PROBLEMS

by
Jane Wallace

Illustrations by
Carole Vincer

KENILWORTH PRESS

First published in Great Britain by
The Kenilworth Press Limited,
Addington, Buckingham, MK18 2JR

© The Kenilworth Press Limited 1994

British Library Cataloguing in Publication Data
A catalogue record for this book is available from the British Library.

ISBN 1-872082-61-0

Typeset by The Kenilworth Press Limited

Printed in Great Britain by Westway Offset, Wembley

CONTENTS

SOLVING
CROSS-COUNTRY
PROBLEMS

4   Introduction
5   Refusing to start
6   Excitability at the start
7   Hanging for home
8   Lost confidence
8   Refusing
10   Running out
10   Hitting fences
12   Strong and pulling
12   Difficulty turning
14   Standing off too far
14   Rider falling off
16   Horse falling
16   Ditch aversion
18   Water aversion
18   Problems with coffins
20   Running into the bottom of fences
20   Combination problems
22   Slow finishing times
22   Remembering the course
24   Final thoughts

Introduction

The majority of cross-country problems can be avoided. A well-trained horse and rider should be able to cope with the various fences found on a typical course, provided they are correctly prepared. This preparation requires both long- and short-term input: in the long-term it involves hours, months and probably years training both horse and rider to compete at a particular level; in the short-term it means the careful walking of the course, and the riding in and warming up necessary for the day's competition.

Most cross-country faults are caused by rider error, and can be avoided by more thoughtful riding. Experience plays an enormous part in not making mistakes – an inexperienced rider will not have the speed of reaction of an advanced rider. Quick responses can avert many potential mishaps but experience takes time to gain. It is important to ride to your own level of experience. Ambition is healthy,

but aim for perfection at one level before progressing to the next.

As with any sport, technique is the key to success. With riding, the security of the rider's seat is crucial. A rider must sit well, with the weight firmly in the heel at all times. A loose seat will be ineffective and will not provide security when the horse makes a mistake, for example if he pecks on landing, or suddenly lurches sideways.

Make sure too that the horse has good grip. It is advisable to use studs, but never use pointed ones in front in case of a fall. Use either small studs or road studs.

Worn shoes are slippery, especially on hard ground. If the horse feels insecure on his feet, he is unlikely to perform with confidence.

Always try to avoid trouble by being a thinking rider. Don't allow problems to develop which then have to be sorted out.

Refusing to start

Refusing to start is a form of napping, and may have a variety of causes. The horse is saying that he does not want to leave the security of the other horses, the horse-boxes and 'home'. Possibly, the horse is rather a 'character' and is nappy generally, but there is always an underlying reason for a horse behaving in this way.

Napping at the start usually indicates anxiety. A young horse may hang for home but is unlikely to stand and rear because he is innocent of what he is being asked to do. An older horse who has competed many times is well aware of what lies ahead, and it may be that a bad experience has made him suspicious.

A confident horse will proceed with his ears pricked, happy to leave the other horses, but a more diffident type may be reluctant to set off on his own. Whatever the reason for napping, the horse is being disobedient by refusing to go forward from the rider's leg. Firm, positive riding lets the horse know that you are determined.

It is important that the horse is not made to feel more panicky than he already is at the prospect of going cross-country. If the rider gets into an anxious state, so will the horse. Often, a pat and an encouraging word will produce better results than shouting and kicking. It is best to keep a nappy horse on the move at the start and try to trick him into setting off by adopting a rather casual approach to it all.

Always use a strong neckstrap on a horse who rears and keep one hand on it in case you lose your balance.

Excitability at the start

It is an all-too-common sight to see horses in a lather at the start, twirling round in a nervous state and evidently agitated at the thought of what is to come. Very often, though, it is the rider who elicits this tension in the horse. By being tense himself, the rider transfers this message to the horse and a vicious circle ensues – the rider is nervous, so the horse is nervous, so the rider becomes even more tense, and so on.

It is vital that the rider tries to stay calm and relaxed before each phase to give his horse confidence that there is nothing to be anxious about. This is not easy to do, especially when butterflies are whizzing round the tummy, but nerves can be overcome with perseverance and experience. You have to apply a little mind over matter – necessary in many instances when dealing with horses. Horses are quick to pick up any 'vibes' so we must learn how to control our natural fear in tense situations. We must also learn how to calm our horses and relax them.

At the start, the rider should ride round on a fairly long rein, with as light a contact as possible. He should pat the horse in a matter-of-fact, positive way. A nervous pat inevitably makes the horse more worried. A brisk trot to get rid of nervous energy, followed by a walk round on a loose rein (if practical) should help settle the horse (and rider!).

If a horse sets off on the cross-country in a state, he will be unlikely to be an easy ride and he will have expended unnecessary energy before he starts.

Hanging for home

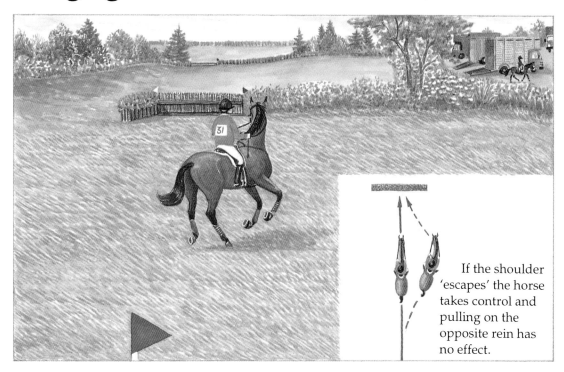

If the shoulder 'escapes' the horse takes control and pulling on the opposite rein has no effect.

There are very few horses who do not hang a little towards home. With strong riding, this presents no problem at all. Some horses are more stubborn about leaving home or their friends and may even veer away from the first fence towards home. This type of horse will take advantage of any weakness in his rider, whether it be a flaw in the training or a lack of determination or ability to control. A horse soon weighs up a situation and realises how effective his rider may be.

A horse probably attempts to hang for home simply because he would prefer not to go. He does not object as violently as the horse who naps and rears. He is testing the rider to see how, or if, he reacts. This is when the rider must nip in the bud any thoughts the horse may have of doing anything other than he is told.

The rider must ride forward strongly, keeping a steady contact with the hand so that the horse cannot deviate from the straight line. In the same way that you pedal faster to correct a wobble on a bicycle, so you send a horse forward to straighten him.

Always remember that a horse leads with his shoulder, so it is useless merely to pull on one rein. The rider must use the outside rein as well as the inside one to keep the horse straight and help turn him. If the outside shoulder 'escapes', the horse takes control and no amount of pulling on the opposite rein will have an effect. The outside aids are important for control, to ensure that the horse is always between hand and leg.

Lost confidence

A lack of confidence can exist in the horse, the rider, or the combination. Confidence takes a long time to build up but can be destroyed in moments. At all times, confidence must be nurtured and safeguarded, for the sake of both horse and rider. If it is lacking in either one, the other will quickly pick up the 'vibes' and feel the same.

One thoughtless act can damage this precious confidence, so try to minimise the risk of making mistakes. Always walk the course carefully and accurately ride the lines you have walked. When cross-country schooling, think carefully about which fences to jump. For example, do not choose a difficult fence as your first fence, however experienced your horse. Always build up to the more difficult obstacles. Never take your horse by surprise; present him correctly at **every** fence, however small. If you ride with your head and so avoid problems, you should be able to keep your confidence buoyant.

To restore lost confidence means going back several stages to re-build it. Return to jumping small fences. Work out why you encountered problems in the first place to avoid a repetition of a bad experience.

Ask an expert for some advice if your training seems to have gone wrong. You and your horse must learn to enjoy cross-country again, so return to a level which you both find easy. If you have a problem with a particular fence, build a replica of it at home if possible, reconstructing it with poles, or go to a schooling course to practise.

Confidence can be rebuilt, but it takes time and patience. Never be in a hurry!

Refusing

There are numerous reasons why a horse refuses at a cross country fence, and it is up to the rider to work out why his horse has stopped to prevent the same mistake from happening again. It is easier to ride over a cross-country fence than over a show jump because the increased pace gives impetus for a wider range of take-off points. The momentum must be replaced by impulsion for show jumping.

The most common reason for a horse refusing is poor presentation at a fence. This includes incorrect pace for the type of fence, i.e. either too fast or too slow; lack of impulsion; incorrect line of approach; loss of balance; horse taken by surprise by too sharp a turn into the fence; lack of determination from the rider; horse slipping on the approach, indicating faulty balance, perhaps caused by incorrect use of, or lack of, studs. The horse may be reluctant to leave 'home', he may be frightened of the fence if he is a young horse, or lacking confidence after a fright if an older one, or he may be in discomfort.

Rider error is unfortunately the main problem. An inexperienced rider will inevitably make more mistakes than an old hand – so, at first, stick to jumping small courses which are more forgiving to the novice.

A horse will not forget a bad experience and will quickly learn how to take advantage of a situation. Make sure that you are well prepared by schooling at home. Take professional advice, even if it is costly.

Always walk the course carefully, and study the line to each fence.

Confidence may be lost after a bad experience.

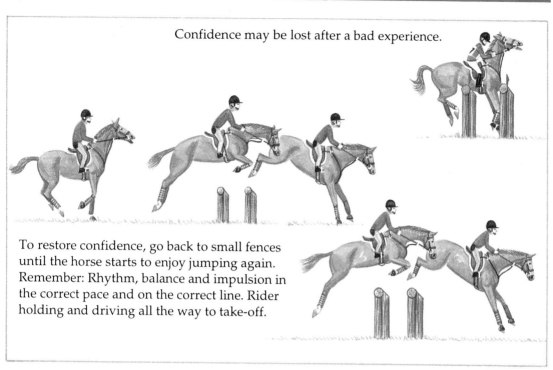

To restore confidence, go back to small fences until the horse starts to enjoy jumping again. Remember: Rhythm, balance and impulsion in the correct pace and on the correct line. Rider holding and driving all the way to take-off.

Running out

The faster speeds in cross-country place more emphasis on obedience and training. The approach to a fence demands greater precision, especially when the terrain increases the degree of difficulty. Many fences are designed so that the horse must jump them on the angle, so offering a greater opportunity for a run-out. Once a horse learns that he can run out, he will quickly realise that it is an easy option when presented with a tricky fence.

Cross-country fences must be tackled from the correct pace for each type of fence and the line of approach must be exact. All lines of approach should be studied carefully when walking the course, with particular attention being paid to corner fences or any fence on an angle. It is useful to line up your intended approach with an object beyond the fence, such as a tree, and plan your route so that you ride into the fence exactly on this line.

Corner fences offer the greatest opportunity for a run-out. The line of approach should arrive at right angles to an imaginary line which bisects the angle of the two rails.

It is important that the horse is schooled at home over a variety of fences on the angle and over corners and narrow fences. Both horse and rider need regular practice over these types of fence. At all times, the rider must insist that his horse jumps a precise point on a fence and not allow him to drift to one side or the other. A strong horse may 'lock' his jaw and run past a fence. This indicates a lack of training and an evasion which has grown into a habit.

Hitting fences

Cross-country fences cannot be knocked down, which means that horses can hit them without incurring penalties unless the horse falls or the rider falls off. Some horses are more careful than others. If a horse regularly hits solid fences he may injure his legs even if he wears protective boots.

Poor presentation to a fence, with an approach which is too fast, lacking impulsion or unbalanced, will give a horse little chance of jumping well. Deep ground or a slippery take-off tests a horse's ability to jump in adverse conditions. Fences in water, difficult distances, undulating terrain, lack of concentration by the horse, as well as a general lack of training, can all contribute to the cause of a horse hitting a fence.

Of course, some fences are easier to jump than others. An upright fence with no ground-line or a flimsily built fence will be difficult for a horse to judge for take-off. It is all the more important that the rider presents his horse correctly with balance, rhythm and impulsion, on the correct line and at the right pace for this type of fence.

Correct training will improve a horse's athletic abilities. The more supple and agile the horse, the more he will be able to cope in an anxious moment. A stiff, unathletic horse will have no option but to hit a fence he meets wrongly because he will be unable to get himself out of trouble. Grids and exercises over fences teach a horse to be nimble and give him the ability to help the rider and negotiate tricky combinations and distances.

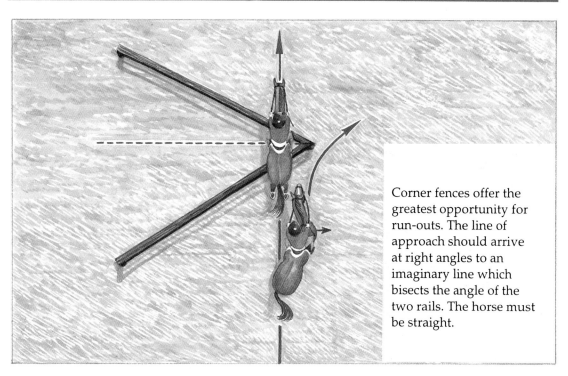

Corner fences offer the greatest opportunity for run-outs. The line of approach should arrive at right angles to an imaginary line which bisects the angle of the two rails. The horse must be straight.

FLAT AND FAST

DROPPING A LEG

Strong and pulling

This is one of the most common problems associated with cross-country. Most horses enjoy galloping and jumping at speed, but this enthusiasm must be controlled and the horse must learn discipline at a faster pace. It is important that a horse is not allowed to go quickly cross-country until his training is established. The moment a horse feels he is in control, the rider will have a difficult task ahead.

The horse must learn to go round a cross-country course at a steady pace – a young horse can be irretrievably spoilt by being galloped round a course before he is mentally ready.

A strong horse whom a rider cannot hold is potentially dangerous. It is vitally important that the rider is in control and able to steady the pace whenever necessary. It may be that a stronger bit will be necessary if corrective training on the flat and over fences does not improve the control. It is difficult to re-school a horse who has learnt that he is stronger than his rider. It is better to prevent the horse from becoming too strong by thorough, correct training.

It is often helpful to use the voice to steady a horse. Good training on the lunge can pay dividends later when riding across country. A firm 'whoa' can work wonders when the brakes fail! Standing up in the stirrups and hauling on the reins does not work – always try to use the correct aids for downward transitions, even at a faster pace. A shorter stirrup helps give a more secure seat on a pulling horse. Always remember, it takes two to pull!

Difficulty turning

Riding cross-country courses puts the horse's training to the full test. In order to turn smoothly and obediently, the horse needs to be balanced, i.e. with his hocks underneath him. As he gallops, the horse drops onto his forehand as the centre of balance moves forward (that is why the rider adopts a forward seat in gallop). In order for the horse to turn easily, he must transfer his weight from his forehand onto his hindquarters. The rider must use the half-halt to achieve this. The better schooled the horse, the smaller the half-halts will need to be. The greener or less educated the horse, the more the half-halts will be needed to re-adjust the balance before making any turn.

Good, basic schooling in every pace will teach the horse obedience to the aids. If the horse is ignorant to the turning aids in trot and canter, he will be even more difficult to turn at a faster pace. It is important to practise plenty of turns onto a straight line in preparation for turning to a fence. It is an easy mistake to fail to straighten the horse fully when turning into a fence. Any lack of control will make it impossible to ride accurate lines to fences. Remember that it is the horse's shoulder which leads, not his head, so it is the outside rein that is most influential in controlling the turn. All too often a rider merely pulls on the inside rein to turn, so losing the horse's outside shoulder. The inside hand directs the horse, but it is the outside aids which bring the horse round, with the inside leg maintaining the impulsion.

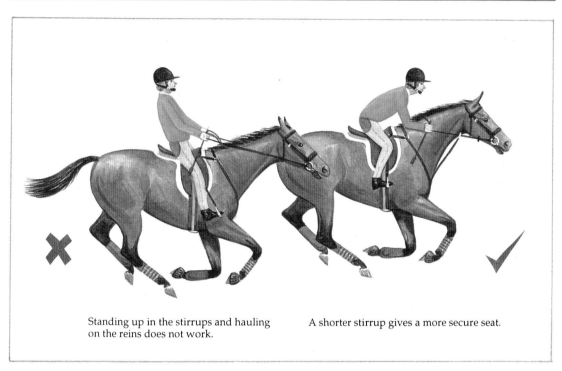

Standing up in the stirrups and hauling on the reins does not work.

A shorter stirrup gives a more secure seat.

All too often the rider pulls on the inside rein to turn so losing the horse's shoulder. Although the inside hand directs the horse, it must be used in conjunction with the outside aids.

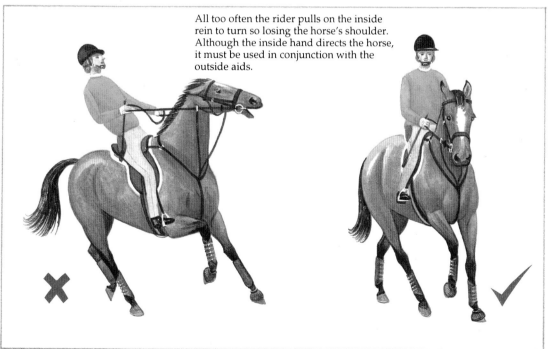

Standing off too far

When a horse stands off a fence invariably it means that he will jump unathletically in a hollow, flat outline.

This will not necessarily cause difficulties over a single, straightforward fence but problems will occur in tricky combinations where the horse must use himself gymnastically. Fences which require the horse to 'pop' will cause trouble because the horse, used to standing off his fences, will be unable to jump from a deeper take-off point. A refusal or maybe even a fall may result.

It is important that the horse jumps as economically as possible, not only to conserve energy, but also to maintain a consistent style of jumping, suitable for the majority of fences. If the rider keeps asking his horse to stand off, the time will come when the horse will be unable to meet his rider's demands. He will try to put in an extra stride and, if unbalanced, will find this impossible so to do.

Gone are the days when event courses comprised straightforward, single fences. Courses now demand a supple, athletic horse capable of jumping at speed, and through combination fences which require true agility.

Many inexperienced riders ask their horses to stand off in their efforts to achieve a fast time. The correct and safe way to ride quickly across country is to maintain an **even rhythm**. Each fence should be approached from the necessary pace for the type of fence and then as soon as the horse has landed, he should be driven quickly back into his stride, and rhythm.

Rider falling off

Every rider is unseated every so often. Jumping at speed over rolling terrain in particular, over drops and through water tests the security of the rider's seat. As discussed earlier, horses can hit solid fences without falling. However, the force of hitting a fence can make a horse peck on landing or screw badly in the air. This effect can be unseating, particularly for the inexperienced rider whose position in the saddle is not yet secure. In moments of crisis a good position can save the day. The rider's weight must be firmly in his heel at all times, and the foot should be braced against the stirrup in case the horse makes a mistake. When jumping a drop fence, the rider must keep his weight in the stirrup with the lower leg slightly forward to absorb the force of the drop. The rider's head must be up and the reins allowed to slip through the fingers as necessary. If this position is automatic at every fence, there is less likelihood of the rider being unseated when the horse makes an error.

If the rider is generally rather sloppy over his position when jumping, not making the effort to keep his heel down and collapsing from habit onto the horse's neck, he will be caught out when the horse jumps awkwardly. When things go wrong, it all happens so quickly that there is no time to think about adopting the correct position – this position must be second nature. A good position is not for mere decoration – it is vital for a secure seat.

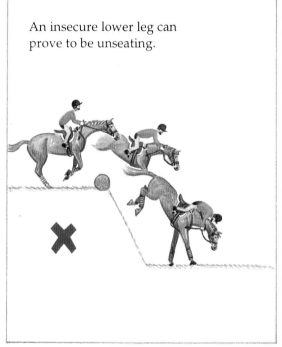

An insecure lower leg can prove to be unseating.

Rider's weight in heel with lower leg forward to absorb force of drop.

Horse falling

Horses do not like to fall any more than we do! All young horses make mistakes and most learn from them. If a horse hits a solid fence hard he will have little chance to stay on his feet. It is the rider's job to present his horse at each fence with the correct approach – in rhythm, in balance and at a suitable pace. The horse must have enough impulsion and be on the correct line.

This gives the horse every chance to jump well. A lapse of concentration, or heavy, sticky or slippery ground can affect how the horse tackles a fence. Adverse conditions such as these place even more emphasis on the rider's ability to present his horse at his fences. There is no margin for error. A well-schooled horse will cope far more easily with difficult conditions than a poorly trained one.

When spectating, you can usually tell when a horse and rider combination is likely to encounter problems. In contrast, a well-schooled pair make everything look so easy. There is no substitute for training and preparation. It entails hours of hard work to consolidate the education of a horse and rider, but without this foundation work, problems are bound to occur at a later stage. It is important that a horse can jump a good show-jumping round and that the rider practises jumping at home and schools cross-county.

The more difficult fences must be treated with respect. Always jump drop fences straight. If a horse drops a leg at such a fence, he will spin sideways and be unable to keep his balance on the other side.

Ditch aversion

Most horses are initially suspicious of holes in the ground. They must learn that there is nothing to fear and be taught how to negotiate them. There are some horses who always detest ditches and remain wary of them all their lives. This type of character will not make a top event horse.

It is important to introduce a young horse to ditches in a progressive way.

Start over tiny ditches, maybe following another horse so that the youngster can build up confidence without being frightened. Gradually he can be asked to jump bigger and deeper ditches, but only when he is quite happy popping over little ones. The horse should be asked to jump them from walk and only progress to trot or canter when he is more experienced.

When a horse has been incorrectly introduced to ditches or appears to be frightened of them, then you should re-school him. You should start at the beginning again, finding a tiny ditch to step over. Grips on the side of the road can be useful, but only if the grass verge is very wide and the road does not carry much traffic. (Never argue with a horse on the road or on a hard, slippery surface.) The horse should be asked to jump a ditch every day until he jumps without hesitation. Only then can he be asked to jump slightly bigger ones. Try jumping him solo, without a lead, but have one ready if required. Jump back and forth over the ditches until the horse jumps with total assurance.

The rider must instil confidence into his horse by riding firmly and positively.

Water aversion

Horses are naturally afraid of water. They cannot know how deep the water is and have to rely totally on their rider. The horse must trust his rider that no harm will come to him and it is the rider's duty never to abuse that trust. The horse must be gradually introduced to water in the same way as with ditches.

Start by walking through puddles and insist that the young horse steps in as many as possible. Give him a lead from another horse if he is suspicious, then make him go on his own. When he is happy, you can introduce him to a bigger stretch of water, but it must not be deep and the bottom must be firm. If the young horse has a fright by stumbling in deep ground or deep water, he may never totally trust water again.

A horse has to learn to accept going into water and the more often he can walk through it, the more confident he will become. Try to practise over different water jumps, always seeking the easiest way in. Try to make the occasion fun and allow him to splash around.

When tackling water jumps in competition, the rider must be firm and determined in his riding. Any hesitation or weakness displayed by the rider will be used as an excuse by the horse. Never take the most difficult route until you are sure that your horse is ready.

If you are eliminated at a water fence, try to go back there for schooling, taking an experienced adviser with you. Provided a horse has been well-educated in water, he should eventually jump it willingly.

Problems with coffins

Coffins are the most influential fences on a cross-country course. Even on the smallest courses where the fences are tiny, the coffin still claims its victims. It is the element of surprise which catches out most horses. Because the rails and ditch are so close the horses have to be not only quick-witted but also quick on their feet. Provided that a horse is happy to jump ditches, is well schooled and is presented correctly at a coffin, the fence should prove to be no problem.

Horses should be taught at home how to cope with the short distances involved in jumping coffins. Working through grids and exercises teaches suppleness and athleticism, vital for the successful negotiation of a tricky fence.

The rider must learn to establish the correct pace for the approach. This is very important, especially after the horse has been in a long, galloping frame. The rider must learn how long it takes to change his horse from gallop to the necessary bouncy canter. A poor approach is the main reason for failure. All too often, the horse is approaching too fast and flat, or with insufficient impulsion. A refusal or a fall is the result. If the approach is too fast, the horse will imagine that he will land in the ditch. If a horse is given a fright by thoughtless riding, it could leave a lasting bad memory.

'Hold' and 'drive' are the key words once the bouncy canter is established. The rider must sit up and stay in behind his horse until he takes off.

If the approach is too fast the horse will imagine he will land in the ditch.

Running into the bottom of fences

When jumping any type of fence, the horse must maintain his rhythm, balance and impulsion until take-off. A horse who loses impulsion during the last few strides will end up creeping into the bottom of his fences. If the horse does not like the look of a fence, he will start to back off. The rider needs to respond by driving his horse forward, otherwise the horse's stride will become shorter and shorter. The resulting jump will be laboured and lacking flow. During a course, this way of going will mean the horse is lacking fluency and rhythm and the rider will have an uncomfortable ride. The horse can manage to scrabble over small fences in this way but will be unable to jump a bigger track.

On the approach, the rider must hold and drive all the way to take-off. If the rider does not keep hold, the horse will quicken and lose balance. This can force him to shorten his stride as he tries to balance himself. The rider must sit up and stay in behind his horse, not leaning forward until the horse has taken off.

When schooling, if the horse creeps into a fence despite all the efforts of his rider, he should be given a sharp smack with the whip on landing. This will teach the horse to stay in front of his rider's leg. It is better to hit a horse after the fence because hitting the horse before the fence can unbalance him and make him jump flat. Also having only one hand on the rein offers an ideal opportunity for the horse to run out.

The rider should always have the feeling that the horse is taking him into the fences. When jumping any fence, the horse should be in front of the rider's leg.

Combination problems

A combination fence should pose no problem to a well-schooled horse, but trouble arises when the horse has not had sufficient basic training. Grids and exercises teach a horse how to use himself and improve his athletic ability.

After a long gallop, the horse's stride is flat and his weight is on his forehand. This must be moved to his hindquarters so that he can shorten his stride and re-balance himself in time for any combination fence. If, through lack of training, or lack of preparation from the rider, this does not happen, the horse is unlikely to be able to negotiate the elements with ease. After jumping uncomfortably several times through combinations the horse will soon begin to associate them with a bad experience and distrust creeps into his mind.

It is the rider's duty to present his horse correctly – this is the purpose of walking the course. The horse does not know what lies ahead, but the rider does.

All distances in combinations should be walked very carefully. All alternative routes should be studied. Do not take the difficult, direct route if your horse lacks experience. If the distance is short and you have had a long gallop leading up to the complex, a major 'gear change' will be necessary. If the distance is long and your horse is short-striding, you know you must arrive with a little more pace.

Combinations are a test of obedience; if problems occur, further training is the answer.

A horse capable of producing a good show-jumping round will find cross-country combinations no problem.

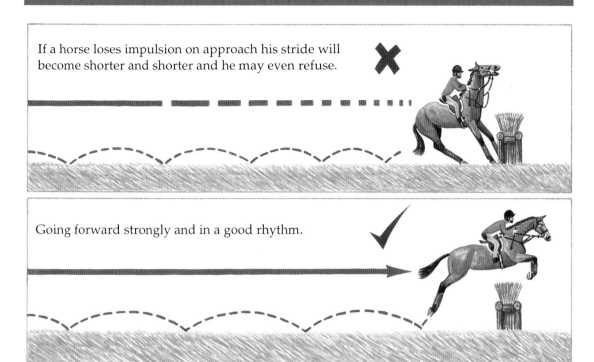

If a horse loses impulsion on approach his stride will become shorter and shorter and he may even refuse.

Going forward strongly and in a good rhythm.

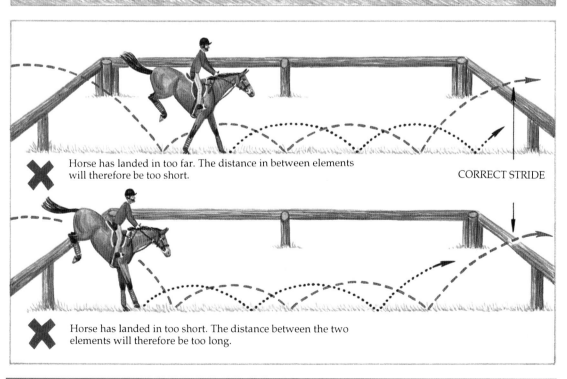

Horse has landed in too far. The distance in between elements will therefore be too short.

CORRECT STRIDE

Horse has landed in too short. The distance between the two elements will therefore be too long.

Slow finishing times

A fast time across country is achieved not by the speed at which the fences are jumped, but by the quickness away from the fences and the economical route taken by the rider. If a horse loses his rhythm at fences, or the rider makes wide turns both into and away from the obstacle, precious seconds will be wasted – multiply these by the number of fences on the course and you can see how much time can be wasted.

Galloping headlong round a course is bad riding which will eventually result in a fall. Instead you should establish a good rhythm and maintain this throughout the course.

Then from a steady pace, you can gradually increase speed without losing balance.

In order to make tight turns, the horse must be well schooled. You should practise at home riding turns into fences and fences on the angle – efficiency here can save valuable seconds.

Study the top event riders and note how they record fast times without appearing to hurry. On their well-trained horses they can alter pace and turn without any resistance, maintaining the same relentless rhythm. A disobedient horse takes a long time to steady and the rider has to start pulling up way before each fence, clocking up extra seconds in the process. A slower, obedient horse will be much quicker round a course than a speedy, ill-disciplined type.

Picking up the rhythm on landing saves valuable time, but both horse and rider must be well balanced to be able to achieve this. A good position is vital if you hope to remain balanced at all times.

Remembering the course

It is easy to lose your way on a cross-country course. The fences are a long way apart and invariably the next fence cannot be seen from the preceding one. You have to be able to memorise which way to turn having jumped a fence, and in the heat of the competition it is sometimes difficult to remember the route.

When walking the course, always take a programme with you and make a note of which way you go after each fence and what landmark to aim for if the fence cannot be seen. As you walk the fences, keep casting your mind back to the beginning and visualise each fence and the route you have taken to and from each one. Do not just think of the fences themselves – they are incidental to the route. Imagine how you will ride to each one, picturing the fence and its approach in your mind's eye.

Before you set off on the cross-country take time to sit down with your programme and carefully go through every fence, every turn and every undulation until you are sure of the way the track takes you. When you are galloping, there is not time to wonder what comes next.

If possible, walk an unfamiliar course more than once. (A three-day event course should be walked at least three times.) The better you know the course, the easier it will be to ride, and the more precise the approaches and lines to the fences will be.

Picture the pattern of the course; take a careful note of where the tricky fences and turns are so both you and your horse can be well prepared.

It's the speed **away** from the fence which helps give a safe, quick time across country.

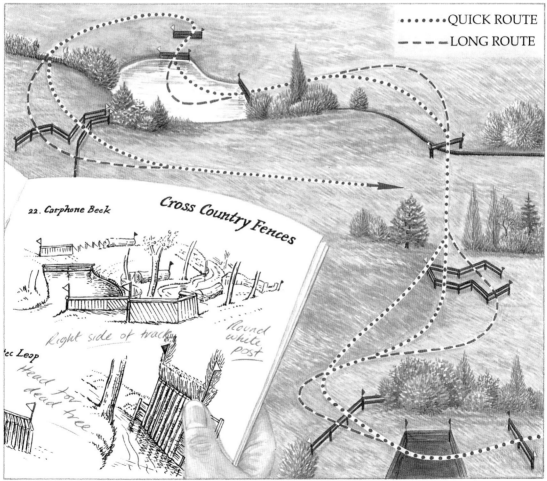

QUICK ROUTE

LONG ROUTE

22. Carphone Beck

Cross Country Fences

Right side of track

Round white post

ec Leap

Head for dead tree

Final thoughts

All the problems which occur cross-country stem from a lack of training. The hours spent on flatwork from an early age will reap dividends when it comes to riding the horse across country. However carefully a horse is produced, it is inevitable that you will encounter at some stage a minor problem associated with cross-country. The key is to prevent this problem from developing into a major one. Do not ignore the first warning signs that all may not be well. If your horse is becoming more and more hesitant at ditches, for example, do not wait for him actually to refuse, but take him schooling to iron out his (or your) worries. If you, yourself, feel anxious about the fences you are jumping, then return to jumping smaller ones until you are ready for bigger ones again. Remember, it should be fun – it should not be a test of nerves.

If your horse is not jumping well at home, he will jump worse in competition. Do not assume it will just 'happen' on the day – good results are proof of correct, thorough training. Winning should not be a case of good luck – it should be the result of hours of schooling, both on the flat and over fences.